independe.
director

Directors' Remuneration

A PRACTICAL GUIDE TO SETTING THE PAY AND BENEFITS OF SENIOR EXECUTIVES

Sub-Editors: Caroline Proud, Lesley Malachowski
Production Manager: Lisa Robertson
Design: Alex Grant
Commercial Director: Ed Hicks
Publishing Director: Tom Nash
Chief Operating Officer: Andrew Main Wilson
Chairman: Miles Templeman

Published for the Institute of Directors, Ernst & Young LLP, Lane Clark
& Peacock LLP and Lawrence Graham LLP by Director Publications Ltd
116 Pall Mall London SW1Y 5ED
020 7766 8950
www.iod.com

This book is part of the Independent Director Initiative (IDI)
from the Institute of Directors and Ernst & Young LLP,
which supports and promotes the role and contribution
of independent non-executive directors.

© Copyright January 2005
Director Publications Ltd
A CIP record for this book is available from the British Library
ISBN 1 9045 2030 8
Printed and bound in Great Britain
Price £9.95

Contents

Except where otherwise stated, this Guide has been written by Ernst
& Young's executive compensation team, with special thanks to Brian
Friedman, Tim Rolfe, Robert Booker, Julian Ingleby and Rupal Patel.

3

New rules, new challenges

Miles Templeman, director general, Institute of Directors

When the first edition of this Guide was published, UK quoted companies were just about to have to comply with the Directors' Remuneration Report Regulations 2002. These regulations set new standards for the level of disclosure by quoted companies and gave shareholders the right to an advisory vote on the remuneration report. It was less than six months before we had the first adverse vote. Directors' remuneration, and particularly 'rewards for failure', have seldom been out of the media or legislative spotlight since.

At the same time as this edition of the guide comes out, the EU Commission is adopting a recommendation on "fostering an appropriate regime for the remuneration of directors of listed companies". Thankfully for those companies, the proposals so closely follow the UK regulations that there will be no need for further action for the UK to comply.

The spotlight has increasingly fallen on the role of the remuneration committee, and the non-executive directors who sit on it. The remuneration committee has to be able to justify itself to all shareholders, not just those who take a considered view. Its task is unenviable. It will, inevitably, be its failings, not its successes, that make the news. Its members will get the flak if an executive director leaves and is perceived to have been rewarded – often whether or not there has been any failure.

Remuneration committees are not short of advice; as with most areas of corporate life, the problem is evaluating it. This

Guide does not attempt to provide simple answers to complex problems. It does, though, give an overview that helps the non-executive directors on the remuneration committee ask the right questions and critically assess the advice they are given.

I commend this Guide to you.

Striking a balance

Gerald Russell, senior partner of Ernst & Young in London and co-chairman of the Independent Director Initiative

Boardroom pay has become the subject of close scrutiny over the past few years. Hardly a week passes without media comment about 'excessive' pay levels or 'unjustified' share option grants. This is not just a problem for the particular companies and individuals under the spotlight: it has a cumulative impact on the public's view of business leaders and business in general.

Scrutiny has intensified at a time when the rules governing boardroom pay have become more stringent. Directors are being urged to make pay arrangements less complex and, under extensive disclosure requirements, easier to understand. Both the Association of British Insurers (ABI) and the National Association of Pension Funds (NAPF), which represent major institutional shareholders, have issued recommendations on boardroom remuneration, focusing particularly on the need for a clear link between total pay and corporate performance over the longer term, and on severance payments. These two organisations are clearly taking a more prescriptive and vocal approach.

The issue of executive pay is of immediate interest to non-executive directors, who are generally expected to exert an independent and moderating influence on salary and bonus levels and to ensure that appropriate performance targets are set.

Good levels of remuneration and incentives and rewards are essential for all those who take on the responsibilities of running companies. In special circumstances, such as when businesses may need rescuing or restructuring, these are always major challenges that can mean a high degree of risk for the individual involved – and remuneration needs to reflect this.

Achieving appropriate pay levels and setting the right incentives is very difficult and requires a great degree of openness and discussion with stakeholders.

As with many things, it is a question of finding the right balance. Directors must be rewarded properly – and they must also be rewarded fairly.

One of the roles of the Independent Director Initiative (IDI), a joint venture between Ernst & Young and the IoD, is to stimulate debate about this subject. This publication is intended to be a contribution to that debate. More importantly, it is also intended to be a tool for the development of good practice within organisations.

Chapter 1

The background

Factors that have influenced boardroom pay over the past quarter century

EXECUTIVE SUMMARY

- changes to the tax regime during the Thatcher years saw a move towards lucrative share option plans

- in the past 12 years, executive pay has come under the scrutiny of five separate corporate governance committees

- institutional shareholder bodies are taking a progressively more prescriptive approach

- the government has intervened to promote transparency and increase shareholder power

Today's executive pay policies originate from the early 1980s when the Conservative government encouraged the adoption of US-style executive remuneration practices. In the ten years up to 1979, successive periods of statutory and voluntary pay controls compressed differentials between executives and other employees.

High marginal tax rates had reduced the incentive effect of cash remuneration increases. Under the first Thatcher administration, marginal tax rates were lowered and new 'approved' executive share option plans were given favourable tax treatment.

The late 1980s saw an escalation in executive pay packages, fuelled by lower inflation, a bullish stockmarket and improving company performance. Base salaries rose; annual bonus plans and share option plans offered the prospect of significant wealth creation for executives in public limited companies.

REVIEWS OF UK PRACTICES

Increasing executive remuneration levels and wider pay differentials have caught the media's attention. The focus on so-called 'fat cats' and 'executive greed' sometimes overshadows a deeper debate on the social issues that arise from a widening gap between the rich (many of whom are not company directors) and the poor in the UK.

The media have also largely ignored, at least until recently, the more substantial discussions about how remuneration has affected the behaviour of executives and the governance relationships between shareholders and boards, and non-executive and executive directors.

The fact that executive reward has, over the past 12 years, been the subject of no fewer than five inquiries by eminent committees, and more than a dozen sets of regulations and guidelines from the government, the Stock Exchange and investor institutions, shows how difficult it has become to reach a conclusion that satisfies all interested parties.

THE HIGGS REPORT

January 2003 saw the publication of the most recent of the governance reports. Known as 'The Higgs Report', Derek Higgs's 'review of the role and effectiveness of non-executive directors' was controversial when first published. His recommendations were portrayed by many in industry as overly prescriptive and impractical.

The report covered a range of issues, including the role of non-executive directors and their independence, and the role and operation of the remuneration committee. The recommendations of the Higgs Report have been incorporated into the Combined Code on Corporate Governance, annexed to the Listing Rules of the UK Listing Authority. Some parts fall within the 'comply or explain' compliance regime of the Code itself and others are appended to the Code as best-practice suggestions. The relevant recommendations of Higgs should be borne in mind as constructive advice on robust and, in parts, leading-edge corporate governance practices.

The boxes on pages 13 and 14 briefly outline the findings of the five main inquiry committees.

INSTITUTIONAL INVESTOR INTERESTS

The inquiry committees have focused primarily on the corporate governance issues associated with directors' remuneration; they have (with the notable exception of the Higgs report) been more cautious as to what defines best practice in terms of the make-up of the executive remuneration package.

By contrast, the Association of British Insurers (ABI) and other institutional investors have taken a progressively more prescriptive approach to executive remuneration policy and practice. Their interest in executive remuneration started with the growth of executive and all-employee share and share option plans in the 1970s and 1980s, and the need to protect shareholders from equity dilution. However, from 1995 onwards, their guidance on executive remuneration expanded significantly to include aspects of contracts, severance arrangements, pay-performance linkage, long-term incentive design, grant levels, grant patterns of all long-term incentive arrangements and market-pay comparisons.

As the representatives of the large UK shareholders, the ABI and NAPF do not guarantee their members' support or rejection of companies' executive remuneration proposals, but their review committees and guidelines are a useful input into remuneration committee deliberations. The fact that the guidelines have expanded in content, and increased in specificity, indicates clearer direct interest by shareholders in setting directors' remuneration.

SHAREHOLDER ACTIVISM

Institutional shareholder activism has been manifest in a number of co-ordinated shareholder votes in the past few years. Marconi, Prudential (itself a member of the ABI) and Sainsbury are all examples of companies where institutional investors have launched concerted attacks on remuneration policy. Company reactions to institutional pressure have been varied. The 2004 AGM season witnessed a growing level of activism, with numerous examples of shareholders expressing concerns either through the media or by refusing to vote for the remuneration report of the company in question. Last year also saw greater focus on ABI 'red top' notices – warnings to institutional investors that a company is falling short of acceptable corporate governance standards.

GOVERNMENT INTERVENTION

In contrast to the 1960s and 1970s, when governments intervened through pay policy to control executive pay, the government emphasis over the past 20 years has been on the taxation environment and wider governance issues.

Despite concerns about the role executive remuneration played in the high-technology boom and bust, and the linking of executive remuneration practices to accounting and company scandals in the US, the response of the UK government has largely been to put further onus on shareholders to deal with the issues. The most recent significant government intervention is the adoption of the Directors' Remuneration Report Regulations (2002).

These regulations were designed to provide a framework of greater openness and further increase shareholder powers. Under the regulations:

- *quoted companies must publish a detailed report on directors' pay as part of their annual reporting cycle. Disclosure requirements both about facts and policies have increased. (See chapter 5, part 1.) The report must be approved by the board of directors*

- *a graph of the company's total shareholder returns over five years, against a broad equity index, must be published in the Directors' Remuneration report*

- *the names of any advisers to the remuneration committee and the fees paid for their services must be disclosed, along with whether they were appointed independently*

- *companies must hold a shareholder vote on the directors' remuneration report at each annual general meeting*

CADBURY, GREENBURY, HAMPEL, TURNBULL AND HIGGS

The Cadbury Committee (1992)

Sponsor: The Stock Exchange

Main recommendations in respect of directors' remuneration:

- all companies should have a remuneration committee made up of a majority of non-executive directors

- the remit of the committee should cover directors' remuneration and the use of plans involving share dilution

- there should be detailed disclosure of the pay of executive directors in annual reports

The Greenbury Committee (1995)

Sponsor: CBI

Main recommendations:

- the remuneration committee should be composed exclusively of independent directors and make decisions on executive remuneration on behalf of the board

- there should be a remuneration committee report in the annual company report disclosing contract, compensation and benefits details for all executive directors. A format for reporting directors' remuneration was established

- employment contracts for directors should not exceed one year

- there should be a set of executive remuneration guidelines in the Stock Exchange listing particulars

The Hampel Committee (1998)

Sponsors: Stock Exchange, CBI, IoD, ABI, NAPF

Main recommendations:

- the broad framework and cost of executive remuneration must be a matter for the board, acting with the advice of the remuneration committee

- Stock Exchange guidelines should be revised and extended

- companies should not be obliged to seek shareholder approval of remuneration reports and directors' remuneration. (The argument was that it would be 'inappropriate' to single out one aspect of company policy for approval in this way)

CADBURY, GREENBURY, HAMPEL, TURNBULL AND HIGGS

The Turnbull Working Party (1999)

Sponsor: Institute of Chartered Accountants

Main recommendation:

- boards should consider "whether human resource policies and performance reward systems support the business objectives and risk management and control system"

The Higgs review (2003)

Sponsor: Secretary of State for Trade and Industry, Chancellor of the Exchequer

Main recommendations:

- greater transparency and accountability in the boardroom

- formal performance appraisal for directors

- closer relationships between non-executive directors and shareholders

- all boards should put in place a significantly more rigorous appointments process

CONCLUSION

The role of remuneration committees has evolved quickly in the past 12 years. Their decisions are now closely tested by shareholders. Understanding how to make sound and acceptable decisions is a competency required of anyone who sits on a remuneration committee today.

Chapter 2

Governance

Remuneration committees are subject to new controls. Belinda Hudson, an adviser on corporate governance and board effectiveness at Mercer Delta Consulting, examines their role and responsibilities

EXECUTIVE SUMMARY

- best practice dictates policy on executive remuneration be determined by a committee of independent non-executive directors

- the board retains ultimate responsibility for the setting of directors' pay and rewards

- in line with the Higgs guidance, the performance of members of the remuneration committee should be reviewed annually

- shareholders now have the right to an advisory vote on the remuneration report

"There should be a formal and transparent procedure for developing policy on executive remuneration and for fixing the remuneration packages of individual directors. No director should be involved in deciding his or her own remuneration."

Principle B.2, The Combined Code on Corporate Governance, the Financial Reporting Council, July 2003.

THE GOVERNANCE FRAMEWORK

Much of the corporate governance framework that has developed over the past ten or so years relates to executive remuneration. The main components of the framework are:

- *the Combined Code on Corporate Governance – 'the Code'*

- *the Directors' Remuneration Report Regulations 2002 – 'the Regulations'*

The Code, annexed to the Stock Exchange's Listing Rules and reviewed and amended by the Financial Reporting Council (FRC), originated in 1992 with the Cadbury committee report, to which was attached a code of best practice. It was developed by further committees, culminating in a single – or combined – code in 1998. The FRC published a revised version of the Code in July 2003 following the Higgs review (see chapter 1, page 14) and a report by Weir Group chairman Sir Robert Smith on the role and responsibilities of audit committees. Part B of the Code is devoted to the subject of executive pay.

The Regulations were introduced by the government to promote greater transparency. They made disclosure rules for quoted companies more stringent.

The Code and the Regulations are supplemented by guidelines from a number of institutional investors and representative bodies. Examples include:

- Guidelines on Executive Remuneration, *published by The Association of British Insurers (ABI)*

- Best Practice on Executive Contracts and Severance, *jointly published by the ABI and The National Association of Pension Funds (NAPF)*

THE REMUNERATION COMMITTEE

The Cadbury report recommended that companies set up a remuneration committee to formulate policy on executive pay. This recommendation is now an established principle of good governance.

COMPOSITION OF THE REMUNERATION COMMITTEE

The Code stipulates that remuneration committees should be comprised wholly of independent non-executive directors so that there is no conflict of interest – real or perceived. The members must be independent of executive management and must not have any business, family or other relationships that could interfere with the exercise of their independent judgment.

The emphasis, however, is not solely on independence. Competence, relevant knowledge and expertise are equally important. This is particularly the case where the chairman of the committee is concerned. The chairman is responsible for leading the committee and dealing with any remuneration-related questions at the AGM. British institutional investors have a strong preference for chairmen who have extensive knowledge of the UK, rather than US or other foreign markets.

FTSE 350 companies are expected to set up a remuneration committee of at least three members; smaller companies are allowed to have committees of just two people.

The annual report should name the members of the committee and detail the frequency of meetings and attendance by directors. The Code also recommends that committee membership is kept under review and refreshed.

The company secretary is normally the secretary to the committee, but in some companies the group HR director assumes this role.

The committee typically meets about four times a year and usually before a main board meeting.

ACCOUNTABILITY

Remuneration committees are constituted as a sub committee of the board and have delegated responsibility for executive remuneration matters. The committee is accountable to the board and can only make recommendations for approval. It is not empowered to make decisions in the board's name or on its behalf.

The board as a whole retains overall responsibility for:

- *agreeing policy*

- *approving remuneration levels for all executive directors*

- *preparing a remuneration report that is subject to shareholders' approval at the company's AGM*

The Code states that the board's chairman "should ensure that the company maintains contact as required with its principal shareholders about remuneration in the same way as for other matters".

The Code also recommends that the remuneration committee should consult the chairman and/or chief executive about proposals relating to the remuneration of other executive directors.

The committee must have clear terms of reference, explaining its role and the authority delegated to it by the board; these terms of reference must be made available on request or on the company's website.

MEMBERS' PERFORMANCE

Members must devote sufficient time to and play an active role in the affairs of the committee. They must provide constructive challenge, exercise proper oversight and make an effective contribution. They must have relevant expertise and continually update their skills and knowledge.

Post Higgs, their performance and contribution are under much greater scrutiny. The Code now provides "that the board should undertake a formal and rigorous annual evaluation of its own performance and that of its committees and individual directors". Continued membership of the committee is dependent on the director continuing to be effective and demonstrating commitment to the role.

RESPONSIBILITIES

The remuneration committee should have delegated responsibility for setting remuneration for all executive directors and the chairman, including pension rights and any compensation payments. It should also, says the Code, recommend and monitor the level and structure of remuneration for senior management, which should "normally include the first layer of management below board level".

PAY PRINCIPLES

The Code sets out principles that the committee needs to take into account in determining executive remuneration.

The main ones are:

- *"levels of remuneration should be sufficient to attract, retain and motivate directors of the quality required to run the company successfully but a company should avoid paying more than is necessary for this purpose"*

- *"the remuneration committee should judge where to position the company relative to other companies" – but should exercise caution in making comparisons in order to avoid an upward ratchet in rewards without any corresponding improvement in performance*

- *the committee should be "sensitive to pay and employment conditions elsewhere in the group, especially when determining annual salary increases"*

- *a significant proportion of executive directors' remuneration should be structured so as to link rewards to corporate and individual performance and align the interests of executives with those of shareholders*

- *the committee should follow Schedule A to the Code – "provisions on the design of performance-related remuneration"*

- *the committee should aim to ensure that poor performance is not rewarded. In particular, it should "carefully consider what compensation commitments (including pension contributions and all other elements) their directors' terms of appointment would entail in the event of early termination". It should also "take a robust line on reducing compensation to reflect departing directors' obligations to mitigate loss"*

- *"notice or contract periods should be set at one year or less"*

SHAREHOLDERS' APPROVAL

The Code states that shareholders should be invited to approve all new long-term incentive schemes and significant changes to existing schemes.

In addition, the government's 2002 regulations require that the report on directors' remuneration is tabled as an ordinary resolution at the AGM for approval by the shareholders. While the vote is advisory only, any significant opposition is likely to attract adverse media coverage and raise questions about the committee chairman's suitability.

REMUNERATION OF NON-EXECUTIVES

The Code states: "The board itself, or where required by the Articles of Association, the shareholders, should determine the remuneration of the non-executive directors within the limits set in the Articles of Association". Some boards delegate this responsibility to a committee that might include the chief executive.

Fees for non-executive directors should, in line with the Code's recommendations, reflect the time commitment required and responsibilities of the role. They should be paid in cash or shares or a combination of both. Remuneration for non-executive directors should not comprise any performance related element or share options as these might jeopardise independence. If a company decides to grant options to a non-executive director against best-practice guidelines then it must seek shareholder approval in advance. In addition, the options should not vest until at least a year after the non-executive director leaves the board.

The Smith Report on Audit Committees, appended to the Code, suggests that particular attention should be given to the remuneration of the audit committee chairman and other members in light of the more demanding nature of their role.

ADVISERS TO THE COMMITTEE

The Code recognises that the remuneration committee might need to draw on advice from executive directors or senior management and external consultants but urges that care is taken. It states that the committee should appoint its own external advisers to minimise any potential conflict of interest. In addition, the Regulations require disclosure of the name of any such consultants and the nature of any other services they have provided to the company.

CONCLUSION

The remuneration committee plays a pivotal role in ensuring that the executive remuneration strategy is aligned with the company's strategy and that pay is linked to performance. To fulfil their role effectively, the members of the committee must have the requisite expertise and knowledge and devote proper time and attention to the issues. Above all else, they must demonstrate competence and independence.

Chapter 3

Getting prepared

Members of the remuneration committee need to do their homework. This section describes what this should involve

---

EXECUTIVE SUMMARY

- the right judgments depend on a full understanding of both the nature and ethos of the business

- in certain circumstances, the committee will need to spearhead a policy review

- the interests of all stakeholders should be key factors in the decision-making process

- market data on executive rewards is not definitive: refer to it but keep an open mind

---

Rewarding executives requires informed judgment. Remuneration committee members do not need expert knowledge, but they do need data to make sound decisions on levels of remuneration, on the link between remuneration and performance, and on the structure and cost of all elements of the executive package.

The starting point is a thorough understanding of the company, normally obtained through a preliminary briefing and perusal of annual reports. But this is seldom enough. This chapter considers the type of information an outside director needs before going to the first remuneration committee meeting and how to place that information in the context of directors' remuneration.

UNDERSTANDING THE BUSINESS

Directors' remuneration levels vary greatly from business to business, as do policies (for example, the performance measures used in incentive plans) and the composition of the package (for example, the balance between short-term and long-term incentives).

The key factors in decision-making are listed below.

business 'size'

Size can affect all aspects of pay – base salary levels, annual bonus design, performance measures and the type of long-term incentive plans that are appropriate. But it is a variable concept. It can be measured in terms of revenues, capital employed, margins or financial structures. Market capitalisation is seldom the main factor in directors' remuneration.

performance record and prospects

Is the company a new business, an established business with a steadily improving performance, a business that is going through a recovery or a turnaround? Are there clear strategic challenges to address? Is it fast-growing with an unpredictable future, or stable with limited but fairly certain prospects?

sector

Both business sector and the position of a business within it are significant. For example, an IT company may operate in a more diverse industry, with many more competitors than, say, a leading supermarket. This should influence decisions about market comparisons and incentive design.

internationalisation, complexity and innovation

Many top UK companies now have non-UK executives on their boards, or in key positions in important subsidiaries that may be based overseas. Should all of the overseas subsidiary companies follow UK pay norms? How should they accommodate US or European pay norms for overseas directors? Should the pay of directors in international, or high-technology, companies differ from that of directors in companies of equivalent size that operate only in the UK, or in low-technology or regulated industries?

cashflow and debt levels

Both these might place an important limitation on smaller organisations where the pay of directors can be a significant proportion of business costs.

key performance measures

These should provide the essential underpinning when it comes to designing incentives, be they short-term or long-term. What are the important performance measures that are associated with increasing shareholder value? How is the company doing in comparison with its competitors on these measures? What are the critical short-term and long-term indicators of performance? Ultimately, performance measures should be based on 'best fit' for businesses.

UNDERSTANDING COMPANY CULTURE AND VALUES

Every organisation has its own culture and values, and these are frequently reflected in remuneration, whether in the design of incentives or the type of benefits available, or, indeed, the level of remuneration itself. Outside directors need to be able to recognise deeply held values that are associated with success and to avoid cutting across these values when it comes to remuneration arrangements. Issues to watch out for include:

■ *attitudes about differentials and fairness. In some organisations, it would be damaging to adopt upper-quartile pay for directors while adopting median-market pay levels for managers. Similarly, it might not be acceptable to the directors, or other employees, to give a pay increase at board level when there is a pay freeze on the shop floor*

■ *founder's values. Many companies are still heavily influenced by the values of their founders. These might distinguish them from their competitors as employers with a particular 'value set' – for example, 'family friendliness' or corporate social responsibility. Directors might be expected to champion these values in the way they work and are paid*

■ *attitudes about ownership. Some companies value share ownership as a philosophy. This might influence the share plans in use not only on the shop floor, but also at executive level*

■ *attitudes about performance measurement. Some businesses have a clear attitude to this – for example, using team not*

*individual measures or being an organisation that priori-
tises 'shareholder value' or 'economic profit'. Directors' incentives that undermine these values can be damaging*

Of course, there will be times when outside directors will have to
challenge current practices. Observing the culture and values of
a well-established and successful business is one thing; 'going
with the flow' for the sake of it is another. If the organisation is
in flux or experiencing rapid change, a decisive shift might be
required. A different approach to executive remuneration – whether
to salary levels, performance targets or longer-term incentives
such as share options – can help change behaviours and shake
up a moribund organisation.

UNDERSTANDING CURRENT ARRANGEMENTS

Remuneration committees are rarely given the luxury of starting
from a clean slate. Before the first meeting, it is useful to get a full
briefing from fellow committee members, the chief executive or the
human resources director. In particular, the committee must know:

- *the overall remuneration philosophy – the positioning of total
  remuneration relative to the market place, the definition of
  the market place, the approach to short-term and long-term
  incentives, the benefits policy, etc*

- *contract details – notice periods, severance arrangements,
  compensation for loss of office, special arrangements (if any)
  in relation to changes of control*

- *details of individual directors' remuneration for the past three
  to five years – including base salary, bonuses, long-term
  incentive grants and exercise values*

- *how far current remuneration complies with ABI and NAPF
  guidelines*

- *any immediate changes planned (for example, as a result of
  the expiry of a share option plan, or a change in the strategy
  of the business)*

- *any special arrangements for individual directors and why they exist. New hires or executives approaching retirement, for example, might have been offered something different*

- *the market information provided by advisers*

- *how outside advisers were appointed, who they are, and why they were selected*

UNDERSTANDING STAKEHOLDER INTERESTS

Within the confines of the law and Stock Exchange listing requirements, directors' remuneration is chiefly a matter for the company, its shareholders and executives. However, decisions are closely watched by a wide range of other people and institutions. Executive pay can come under fire when an interest group's view of the company clashes with the way the board is being rewarded. As a result, understanding interest groups and their perceptions of the company is vital in ensuring smooth implementation of remuneration committee recommendations. The main interest groups are:

- *major shareholders. In companies that are majority owned by an individual or family, there are usually specific issues to address surrounding share dilution or payments made to executives who are also family members. Even in companies where share ownership is spread much wider, there might be a few influential institutional shareholders who need to be involved in discussions of big changes in remuneration*

- *smaller shareholders. Small shareholders might lack the voting muscle to obstruct remuneration decisions, but they might still be able to make considerable 'noise' in the press or in a local area. Companies jealous of their community reputation, or those with large numbers of shareholders who are also customers (such as privatised utility companies and demutualised financial services organisations), might need to consider small shareholders' views on directors' remuneration*

- *institutional investor organisations. Organisations such as the ABI, NAPF and the Pensions and Investment Research*

Consultants (PIRC) play a major role in setting the frame-work for directors' remuneration. They, and their members, can launch concerted action against pay proposals. Now that remuneration reports are subject to shareholder approval (albeit only an advisory vote), their 'activism' is increasing

■ *the directors. Understanding how executives view their own remuneration is useful. If it is not appropriate to talk to them directly, it might be sensible to ask the remuneration com-mittee's advisers to undertake a review. If remuneration policies are intended to attract, retain and motivate executives it is worth knowing whether or not they are appreciated*

■ *employees and unions. Employees and their union represen-tatives often express no views on executive remuneration, but in certain circumstances are likely to be vocal. There needs to be special consideration of directors' remuneration where there are significant redundancies or pay freezes for other staff*

■ *the media. Some journalists watch executive remuneration closely. If the company has recently been in the press over its directors' remuneration, close media attention will probably continue. The experiences of (among others) British Gas, Vodafone and GlaxoSmithKline illustrate how difficult it is to shake off press interest*

■ *government and regulatory interests. Certain industries and organisations attract attention from the government and regu-latory bodies such as the Financial Services Authority. It is important for remuneration committees to understand how their decisions might be influenced by these stakeholders*

Perceptions of a company and its directors' remuneration can change very quickly; a reasonable decision made one year might be unacceptable the next.

In the current environment, remuneration committees can be publicly challenged on their judgments. These judgments often weigh a large number of variables, and inevitably others might take a different view. Knowing who else is going to form their own view,

MAIN SOURCES OF MARKET DATA		
Source	**Advantages**	**Disadvantages**
Published data from annual reports	Readily available either individually or in survey form. Named companies and individuals.	Insufficient detail and job analysis. Information might be out of date.
Published surveys	No participation required. You can buy what you want.	No control over design and content. You usually get limited job inform -ation. Data are often not comprehen -sive (for example, long-term incentive details and benefits information may be missing).
Consultancy surveys	Large databases, detailed analysis. Can often provide specific cuts of data to suit company needs.	Lack of control over design and content. Further analysis might be costly.
Bespoke surveys	You design the survey and own the data.	Expensive and time -consuming. Will the companies you want participate?
Personal contact with non-executives other companies	Confidential information that might not be available through formal surveys.	Information might be incomplete or selective. Not usually statistically valid.

and how they will react to decisions made, is a key part of the decision-making process.

Most companies look for at least two sources of data to provide a broad picture of the market. The box above and those on the next two pages give a checklist of questions to help judge the quality of the market data and analyses used by a remuneration committee.

UNDERSTANDING THE MARKET

The final element of preparation is to understand markets and market data. Both the Greenbury and Hampel reports made much of the use and abuse of data, and cautioned remuneration committees to take particular care in their use of surveys.

However, market data is an important input into remuneration committee deliberations. Without proper data:

■ *pay levels might not be sufficient to recruit or retain the talent to run the business*

■ *costs might exceed those of competitors and attract shareholder criticism*

■ *differentials between individuals might be harder to justify*

■ *the balance between basic salary and incentives might be out of line, resulting in performance being under- or over-rewarded*

There are various sources of market data. The table on the opposite page lists the main ones and gives a brief analysis of their strengths and weaknesses.

While survey data is often easy to obtain, it seldom gives a definitive picture. Different analytical and valuation methodologies may well give different results. It is not always possible to get

---

QUESTIONS TO ASK ABOUT MARKET DATA

1. Are the right companies in the market sample?

■ Are enough organisations covered? There should be at least 11 to get a statistically valid sample for quartile analyses.

■ Are the relevant organisations in the sample? They should be comparable in terms of sector, size, scope and, possibly, location. A simple test is to ask: "Would we recruit people from these companies?" "Are we at risk of losing directors to these companies?" Watch out for companies that have been omitted – if so, check why.

■ Are the companies in a similar market? International comparisons are normally only valid if the executives have genuine international market value.

QUESTIONS TO ASK ABOUT MARKET DATA

■ Are the companies in a similar performance bracket? Watch out if those in the sample are bigger, or have a better record.

■ Are the companies relevant to the particular executive you are looking at? It might be appropriate to have different comparators for different roles. Jobs such as human resources director or finance director are often less sector-specific than a retail operations director or a director of engineering.

2. Are the right posts in the sample?

■ Are there enough job holders? While the number of organisations in the sample might be sufficient, there might be fewer matches for some jobs.

■ Are the jobs comparable? A company can have a unique organ-isational structure at the top.

Check that the comparisons are like-for-like. There are certain cases where jobs are very difficult to match. These include: chairman and chief executive roles where there are part- and full-time chairmen and some combined chairmen and chief executives; divisional chairmen where there are large differences in the sizes of divisions; chief operating officers where the role is very specific to the organisation; company secretaries, where the role is either purely administrative or more managerial, involving the overseeing of a number of legal, regulatory and other head-office functions.

3. Is the analytical method sound?

■ How has company or job size and complexity been used to 'weight' the analysis? Most survey providers have their own method of weighting company and job size in arriving at the market statistics. Typically, they use a statistical multiple regression technique, group data by turnover size, or employ some job evaluation process. It is important to test how this has affected the data presented.

■ Is there sound data for all jobs? It might be that some jobs have been difficult to match. Check if some data has been provided through 'slotting' of information.

■ Is there a statistical distribution shown? Normally, the analyses should show the median, lower quartile and upper quartile. If these are absent then it might indicate a small sample.

QUESTIONS TO ASK ABOUT MARKET DATA

4. Is the whole package analysed?

■ Is there information on all aspects of remuneration? Market information should include base salary, annual bonus (actual payments, on-target amounts and maximums), long-term incentives (values at grant), benefits (this might be in the form of a features analysis and a calculated value). Often, the analyses may cover: base salary, total cash (base salary and annual bonus); total direct compensation (base salary, annual bonus and value of long-term incentives); total remuneration (base salary, annual bonus, long-term incentive value and benefits value).

information for a precise set of companies. Furthermore, for some organisations, it is very difficult to define the right group of comparators.

Using market data is not a science. It does not provide a right answer and in some cases – for example, where there is a unique, incomparable job – there is no right answer. If the results of your analysis don't 'feel right' they are probably wrong. Market data is there to be questioned and interpreted. It defines the parameters of normality – the boundaries of what is reasonable.

CONCLUSION

Remuneration committees need to have a thorough understanding of their company and the forces that shape directors' remuneration. The preparation above, along with knowledge of the legal framework, the Stock Exchange listing requirements and the ABI and NAPF guidelines, will ensure an informed input to discussion.

Chapter 4

The package

PART ONE: BASE SALARY

'Basic pay' remains the core component of executive reward. Setting it requires careful thought

EXECUTIVE SUMMARY

- salary is increasingly decided case-by-case using market matching; formal, predetermined pay ranges are less common

- pay levels should reflect both the nature of the business and the nature (ie. skills, responsibilities and geographical location) of the director

- the pay gap between executives and other employees must not be unfairly large

- companies must be able to justify salaries that are above the 'market rate'

The annual base salary is the fundamental element of the executive remuneration package. Other elements of variable pay are frequently measured as multiples of base salary, including on-target and annual bonuses and the value of long-term incentive awards. Base salary is also a major factor in determining the cost to the company of providing long-term pension benefits to an individual director. Consequently, the setting of base salary is a key determinant of both current and future costs of employment. The bar chart opposite shows the make-up of the remuneration package of a typical mid-FTSE 250 CEO.

INDIVIDUAL FACTORS

Base salaries of individual directors vary across market sectors and will reflect the size and complexity of the business, the range and nature of individual responsibilities, and each executive's specific skills, competencies and performance. Companies are increasingly

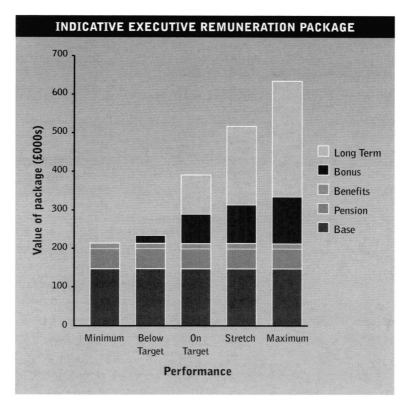

INDICATIVE EXECUTIVE REMUNERATION PACKAGE

setting the pay of directors individually, in order to ensure that the market worth of each director is reflected in base salary.

MARKET RATES

A critical first step in developing a reward framework for executives is to understand the relevant external market. A variety of market surveys and other pay information and analyses is available (see chapter 3). Remuneration consultants will understand the latest pay trends in different markets and for different roles and will be able to comment on typical market increases.

SALARY REVIEWS

Directors' base salaries are typically reviewed once a year. In quoted companies, the review is carried out by the remuneration committee. In private companies, the salaries of senior employees are usually reviewed by the chief executive or chairman and then approved by the board. When setting or reviewing base salaries the following should be considered:

■ *the external competitiveness of base salaries and typical executive salary increases*

■ *specific labour market issues such as skills shortages*

■ *differentials between the pay of executives and the pay of other employees*

■ *individual roles, skills, competencies and performance levels*

■ *base salaries within the context of the total remuneration package, considering variable remuneration levels*

EXTERNAL COMPETITIVENESS

Several organisational factors typically influence base salary:

■ *the size of the company as measured by turnover or market capitalisation*

■ *the geographic spread of the business*

■ *business type*

■ *the function of the job*

■ *external competitiveness*

It is common for companies to use a specific group of comparable companies when benchmarking base salary levels. The comparator group might include companies operating in the same industrial or geographic sector or companies of similar size.

Most institutional investor guidelines in the UK recommend the use of comparison and relativity in remuneration policy and practice. For example, the guidelines on executive remuneration published by the Association of British Insurers (ABI) say that:

■ *remuneration should reflect market requirements, given business size, complexity and geographical location*

■ *when setting salary levels, remuneration committees should consider the market, competitive forces in the sector and the particular challenges for the company*

■ *companies should not 'ratchet up' remuneration unnecessarily by paying more than is required to attract, retain and motivate key employees, including directors*

■ *where a company seeks to pay salaries at above median levels of its comparator group, this should be justified in the remuneration report*

The remuneration committee must bring its independent judgment to bear when deciding whether to pay an individual at the top, middle or bottom of a market salary range.

INTERNAL RELATIVITIES

The remuneration committee and the board should also review the company's internal relativities, keeping in mind that certain roles and geographic markets carry base salary and total cash premia.

Main board directors based in a country where higher levels of remuneration are the norm need to be appropriately rewarded if their services are to be retained. This might mean paying certain divisional heads more than the group chief executive.

Traditionally, companies had fixed pay differentials and/or job evaluation systems that determined the gaps between directors' pay and that of other senior executives. Many companies have also used formal base salary ranges, with directors appointed low in the salary range and their pay rising in relation to individual performance and experience in the post. However, the use of formal salary ranges is in decline.

OWNER-MANAGED COMPANIES

Owner-managed companies often have specific issues in the management of base salaries. The proprietor can earn significant dividends from his/her stake in the company. Consequently, he or she might take a lower base salary than the 'going' rate. It is important that this does not distort the company's view of executive pay: salaries for other directors may need to reflect the wider executive pay market.

NON-EXECUTIVE DIRECTORS' PAY

Key issues

- *non-executive directors are paid fees*

- *even though non-executive directors are expected to exercise independent judgment, their legal responsibilities are the same as those of executive directors*

- *the Combined Code recommends that "the terms and conditions of appointment of non-executive directors should be made available for inspection" and that "the letter of appointment should set out the expected time commitment"*

- *the majority of companies review the fees of non-executive directors annually. However, increases tend to be made less frequently, typically every second or third year*

- *a number of companies is moving to a disaggregated fee approach, for example a basic fee, a fee for serving on each committee, and a fee for acting as chairman of a committee. This reflects the basic premise that time and responsibilities should be the main determinants of fees*

- *some companies pay an additional amount for each board or committee meeting attended. This, however, is not expected to become standard practice. Additional fees are usually only paid when the meeting is held away from an individual's country of residence*

- *a minority of companies currently award part or all of their non-executive directors' fees in company shares. However, this, is controversial (see 'remuneration of non-executives', chapter 2). There are legal complications: the level of non-executive director remuneration in any one year is restricted by the Corporate Articles of Association*

- *the role of the senior independent director (SID) has been enhanced by the Higgs report. Accordingly, fees paid to SIDs might rise in coming years*

- *the new independence rules mean that some deputy chairmen of audit and remuneration committees will be 'unqualified' to assume the role of chair. As a result, remuneration policies for deputy chairmen might become more diverse*

INDICATIVE NON-EXECUTIVE DIRECTORS' FEES (£)						
	FTSE 100			FTSE 250		
	Chairman	Deputy/vice chairman	Director	Chairman	Deputy/vice chairman	Director
Basic fees	200,000	70,000	35,000	100,000	40,000	28,000
Committee fees	Member		Chairman	Member*		Chairman
Audit	5,000-7,000		7,500-12,000	–		5,000
Remuneration	5,000		7,250	–		5,000
Nomination	3,000		5,500	–		3,000

* committee fees are not typically paid by the FTSE 250.

Sources: company annual reports; Non-Executive Director Practice and Fees, Monks Partnership, March 2004.

PART TWO: ANNUAL BONUS PLANS

This section describes the factors that should influence the design of cash awards for good performance

---

EXECUTIVE SUMMARY

■ well-designed bonus plans can be the driving force for improved year-on-year business performance

■ the right performance measures and targets are vital

■ shareholders are increasingly opposed to generous rewards for below-target performance and to uncapped bonus plans

■ deferred bonuses can align corporate and individual interests over the medium term

---

The annual cash bonus is the most common way of providing a short-term incentive to executive directors and other senior managers. Bonus plans are normally intended to:

■ *motivate individuals to achieve the desired levels of performance over the short term*

■ *reward contribution and performance*

■ *align the personal interests and wealth of the executive with the achievement of corporate objectives*

■ *enable executives to share in corporate success, thereby encouraging them to stay with the company*

■ *ensure that the levels of total cash compensation (ie. base salary plus bonus) are competitive*

LIFECYCLE OF THE PLAN

Typical practice in the UK is to construct bonus plans for a 12-month period – in line with the company's financial reporting cycle – so that year-on-year performance improvements can be targeted and rewarded. The annual cycle involves setting performance targets at the beginning of the year, monitoring performance against them during the year, and evaluating performance at the end of the period in order to determine bonus payments.

Most annual plans pay all or part of the bonus in cash following the year-end.

Increasing numbers of companies operate bonus plans for senior executives that include a deferred element, payable in shares after a holding period or subject to the fulfilment of further medium-term criteria. Deferred bonus arrangements are discussed later in this chapter (pages 43 and 44).

TOTAL CASH COMPETITIVENESS

The remuneration committee or board should determine the level of base salary plus annual bonus payment in the context of the company's comparator group. The committee should ask: how does our total cash compensation compare? Account should be taken of varying levels of corporate performance across the comparator group.

Looking at how the company compares with the comparator group on a range of headline performance metrics (such as revenue and earnings growth, capital efficiency and return to shareholders) can provide a view of relative performance. Levels of total cash compensation should generally reflect corporate performance.

Establishing the desired level of total cash competitiveness gives the remuneration committee a starting point for deciding bonus levels, usually expressed as a percentage of base salary.

SETTING PERFORMANCE MEASURES

The success of the bonus plan in influencing the behaviour of participants hinges on the performance measures and targets. These must be carefully selected to reflect business objectives and shareholder value creation. Remuneration committees and boards must ensure the right balance of corporate, divisional and personal performance measures.

corporate performance measures

For executive directors in FTSE 350 companies, typical corporate performance measures are group profitability, earnings per share growth, economic value added, cashflow or return on capital. In smaller companies, typical practice is to use a performance measure based on corporate profitability – the measure is normally calculated as profit before tax, excluding exceptional items and amortisation of goodwill.

divisional performance measures

The most common measure of divisional performance for corporate directors with line responsibilities for company divisions is divisional profit, return on capital or cashflow. These measures are often combined with corporate measures in the annual bonus plan to reflect directors' responsibilities for both corporate and divisional performance.

individual performance measures

Where used, individual performance measures are normally either quantifiable and role-related or discretionary, requiring a more qualitative evaluation of the executive's performance and contribution. Where a particular business outcome is strategically key, bonus payments for the achievement of appropriately selected strategic 'milestones' are not uncommon.

For executive directors, individual performance measures, if present at all, usually constitute only a small proportion of the bonus plan entitlement. In some companies, bonuses related to personal performance might only be paid if corporate performance targets have been met to at least some degree.

balanced scorecards

A few companies use a scorecard of measures in annual bonus plans, mixing both qualitative and quantitative indicators. Measures such as customer and employee satisfaction, health and safety performance, corporate social responsibility and achievement of specific strategic milestones might be included, alongside the personal and financial measures described above. The balanced scorecard approach can be effective in bringing a strategic dimension to annual bonus plans, but can be difficult to operate.

PERFORMANCE TARGETS

In addition to making decisions about performance measures, the remuneration committee or the board needs to set performance targets for the bonus plan. Typical plan design is based on three levels of performance:

■   *threshold (the lowest level at which a bonus becomes payable)*

■   *on-target (the level of performance expected)*

■   *the level at which the maximum bonus will be earned (although it should be noted that some organisations do not operate a bonus cap).*

threshold performance

The remuneration committee and the board should decide whether it is appropriate to reward performance that is marginally below target. This decision will partly depend on the level of 'stretch' in the target itself. The committee and board should also consider the amount of bonus (perhaps denominated as a percentage of base salary) that should be paid for this level of achievement.

Recent pressure from institutional investors suggests that reward for achievement of targets below market expectations should be extremely modest.

on-target performance

The key consideration is the level of performance required for an on-target bonus to be paid. Current practice in the UK suggests that performance targets should be stretching, not merely linked to a budget number.

The remuneration committee should consider the level of stretch within performance targets in determining the associated level of bonus payment. At the time of writing, for FTSE 250 companies an on-target bonus of around 30 per cent of base salary is typical. For larger companies, especially those that are truly global and/or in the financial sector, higher on-target bonuses can be expected. Higher levels of on-target bonus might also be appropriate for directors located in countries where bigger bonuses are more common.

performance level for maximum bonus

A company must decide on the level of any bonus cap and specify the circumstances in which the maximum would be paid. If the remuneration committee or the board believes that no cap should apply, it should consider the levels of superior performance required for additional bonus payouts. Consideration should also be given to shareholders, which increasingly oppose uncapped bonus plans.

At the time of writing, bonus maximums among the FTSE 250 are often around 70 per cent of base salary. Potential bonuses are higher in FTSE 100 organisations and those businesses, sectors and countries associated with higher bonus payments.

BONUS PROFILE

By setting the levels of performance required for threshold, on-target and maximum bonus, a bonus profile can be developed. Commonly, there is a straight-line relationship between on-target performance and the performance level for the maximum bonus; for every one per cent increase in performance, there is a fixed 'y' per cent increase in bonus payout (see 'A' opposite). However, if greater importance is attached to achieving at least on-target performance, the gradient of payments between minimum and on-target should probably be steeper than that between target and maximum (see 'B' opposite). To provide a clear incentive for achievements above on-target performance, the reverse might be appropriate – ie. a steeper gradient between target and maximum (see 'C' opposite).

EVALUATION OF PERFORMANCE

At the end of the performance year, an assessment must be made against chosen criteria, and levels of bonus calculated. For exec-

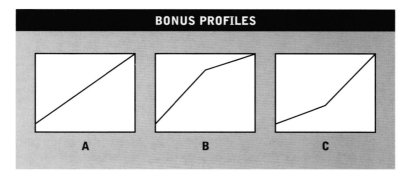

BONUS PROFILES

A   B   C

utive directors of quoted companies, bonus payments are normally approved by the remuneration committee or the board and are subject to audit.

In assessing performance, the committee or the board might wish to consider any exceptional circumstances that have arisen during the year, although it is important to maintain the integrity of the plan.

Where individual performance is a factor determining the level of bonus, an assessment of personal performance must also be undertaken.

DEFERRED BONUSES

The design of deferred bonus plans varies widely, involving either compulsory or voluntary deferral of a proportion of the bonus (or a mixture of these). The deferred proportion is typically used to purchase company shares, which are then held in trust for a period of time, most commonly three years. Under some deferred bonus plans, an additional 'matching' payment might be made at the end of the deferral period, again often provided in the form of equity. Institutional investors prefer that equity provided by companies on this matching basis is subject to ongoing performance conditions over the deferral period.

Under an illustrative deferred bonus plan, executives might be required to defer 50 per cent of any bonus entitlement, and may defer other amounts if they wish. In both cases, deferred bonus is invested on the executive's behalf in company shares. In return for such deferment, the company may provide up to one matching share for each share purchased with the deferred bonus. The actual level of matching is determined by performance over three years against a fixed benchmark or measure.

Deferred bonus plans are often used as a retention tool (whereby the executive forfeits the additional element of the deferred bonus on resignation).

They can also increase alignment between the wealth of executives and the creation of shareholder value by encouraging executives to build up a personal holding of equity in the company.

ANNUAL BONUSES IN SMALLER COMPANIES

Particular care needs to be taken in annual bonus design for smaller companies, where cashflow is a critical performance measure, or where bonuses might amount to a significant proportion of total costs. If the performance measures used don't directly link to profits or cashflow, it might be necessary to allow for deferment or non-payment of bonuses if the financial health of the company means payments cannot reasonably be made.

DESIGN REVIEWS

As with all areas of remuneration, design practice is constantly evolving and innovations are emerging. Advice should be sought periodically to ensure that both bonus levels and bonus design continue to support the strategy of the business.

PART THREE: LONG-TERM INCENTIVE PLANS

The design of tools to reward performance over time is becoming increasingly more complex

EXECUTIVE SUMMARY

- long-term incentive plans must form a balanced part of the total remuneration package
- performance targets should be clear, measurable and realistic and reflect strategic needs
- regard should be paid to changes in tax and accounting rules
- the interests of institutional investors should be borne in mind: follow their guidelines

Awards under long-term incentive plans are primarily made to motivate and encourage directors and other key members of senior staff to focus on creation of shareholder value.

Long-term incentives now make up a significant part of a senior executive's total remuneration package (see the bar chart on page 33). They can play an essential role in the recruitment of an executive and in ensuring that their services are retained.

Long-term incentives can take the form of cash or shares. For larger, listed companies, institutional shareholders and their representative bodies prefer awards of shares (or an interest in shares) to be made to executives. This ensures that the interests of shareholders and the executives are more closely aligned.

Smaller businesses and private companies might not have a ready market for their shares and are more likely to make long-term awards of cash. A cash-based plan might also be preferred by some subsidiaries of public limited companies to maintain a close focus on the results of the particular business.

Although awards under long-term incentive plans are generally greater than those under annual bonus plans, the performance criteria tend to be more stretching and rigorous.

BEST PRACTICE

The potential value of long-term incentives has attracted considerable attention in the media in recent years. Long-term incentives have increasingly become a focus of shareholder activism – particularly since the introduction of new reporting requirements. Listed companies are closely scrutinised by institutional shareholders and must give serious consideration to the guidelines of those investors and of organisations such as the ABI. The following are key points for the remuneration committee:

- *the award of a long-term incentive must be seen as part of the executive's total remuneration package. When setting the value of an award, due attention should be paid to the salary, annual bonus, benefits and pension arrangements of the executive group*

- *regardless of whether the award is in the form of shares or cash, any performance conditions must be linked primarily to the long-term performance of the company and reflect the business and human resources strategy*

- *performance targets should be measurable and understandable; in order for a long-term incentive plan to be motivational, the executives must feel that the targets are attainable and clear and that they can influence their achievement*

- *accounting cost and valuation issues, as well as corporation tax deductions, must be taken into account at an early stage of the planning process*

PLAN DESIGN

The design and implementation of a long-term incentive plan can be complex. It is an area where companies and their remuneration committees might wish to take advice from specialist consultants. In addition to the human resource and corporate governance aspects, companies must be aware of the potential legal, tax and National Insurance consequences of making long-term incentive awards. Additionally, there might be accounting costs and tax implications – these are discussed more fully in the last section of this chapter.

Things get even more complex when more than one country is involved. Design and implementation across national boundaries require in-depth knowledge of international regulatory and tax regimes.

SHARE PLANS

Unlike all-employee share plans, executive long-term incentive plans that use shares cannot generally receive Inland Revenue approval. Accordingly, there is greater scope for flexibility in their design; many different types of share-based long-term incentive plans are in use. The most common are executive share options, enterprise management incentives and restricted share plans.

executive share options

Executive share options usually work in the same way as Inland Revenue approved share option schemes but allow for far larger grants of options. The maximum value of options under the Inland Revenue approved element of a plan is currently £30,000. This limit has remained unchanged for a number of years.

Market practice on share option grants has evolved considerably in recent years and continues to move on. We used to see single lump-sum grants of share options with a face value of the underlying shares, of up to four times basic salary. Now, annual grants of executive options are the norm.

Face values of between 100 per cent and 300 per cent of salary each year are not unusual.

Over the years, annual grants create a portfolio of options at different exercise prices. The size of option grants depends on the company's size and the performance conditions attaching to the exercise of the options. Also, norms vary by sector. In the UK, executive share options are typically not exercisable until three years after grant and until stretching performance conditions have been met. Performance norms are closely prescribed by institutional shareholder guidelines.

Enterprise Management Incentives (EMIs)

The Finance Act 2000 introduced Enterprise Management Incentives, a share option plan for companies with gross assets of no more than £30m. The business of such companies must be a qualifying trade – property development companies or financial services companies are among those excluded.

EMIs have proved to be popular benefits, mainly because the shares acquired are taxed as capital gains rather than income.

restricted share plans

In the late 1990s, restricted share plans (often referred to as long-term incentive plans or LTIPs) became more common as executive incentives in the UK, either as substitutes for, or in addition to, share options. Restricted share plans work in conjunction with an employee benefits trust, which acts as a warehouse for the shares. Unlike share options, they are usually acquired for no payment.

The award to an executive will only vest after time (typically three or five years) and only after stretching performance conditions are met. The vesting of restricted share awards is usually subject to more challenging performance conditions than those attaching to options, with only a small proportion of the share awards vesting for average performance. Institutional investor guidelines are published for these plans.

CASH PLANS

For companies that do not choose, or are not able, to make awards of shares, long-term incentive plans may be cash-based. Where the value of the award is linked to the growth in the value of a company and presented as a 'unit', cash-based plans are often referred to as 'phantom' share plans.

'Phantom' share plans can replicate many of the features of a real share-based plan. The crucial issue is valuation. A valuation model for awards should be linked to business projections and reflect performance in relation to strategic objectives. Companies using cash plans should ensure that:

■   *sufficient cash is generated for payments*

■　*there is an appropriate limit on the proportional share of any increase in shareholder value available to members of the plan*

PERFORMANCE MEASURES

Long-term incentive awards are usually linked to a suitable measure of corporate performance. Some measures are generally accepted by institutional investors and are frequently used by larger, listed companies. Smaller or private companies must pay regard to their business plans when deciding on a relevant performance measure.

Institutional investors are in broad agreement that two types of performance measures are acceptable for long-term incentives:

■　*financial measures, such as earnings per share improvements over the retail price index*

■　*total shareholder return measures relative to a comparator group or index*

While these are currently the most common performance metrics, a wide variety of indicators, and combinations of indicators, is used. It is important that the measures selected are relevant and appropriate to the company and its executives.

Remuneration committees should always be aware of the views of major investors when deciding on performance measures and rewards for different target performance levels. A dialogue with those investors often allows a company to resolve contentious issues privately.

DILUTION

Institutional investors in the UK wish to encourage employee share ownership, but are always concerned that the interests of existing shareholders should not be diluted excessively by the grant of options, or other share rights to employees. From time to time, they publish guidelines, recommending limits on dilution caused by all share plans (currently ten per cent in ten years) and executive plans. While these guidelines do not apply to unquoted companies, they are an important benchmark.

RECENT DEVELOPMENTS

Recent 'technical' developments are forcing companies to consider the value offered to participants in equity incentive plans, as weighed against potential administrative and financial costs. The most important developments relate to accounting and taxation.

accounting

The introduction of international accounting standards (IFRS 2 and the UK equivalent FRS 20) means that companies must recognise an expense for share-based payments in the income statement. The real impact of IFRS 2 and FRS 20 will be on employees' and directors' share options and other share-based incentives. Employers need to consider the impact of the accounting expense, and whether that expense can be justified in terms of the value perceived by, and delivered to, employees relative to their cost.

corporation tax

Legislation relating to the provision of shares or options was introduced in 2003. The rules aim to provide symmetry between the income tax due and the corporation tax relief available. Where certain conditions are met, a corporation tax deduction should be available for providing share options, but it will not apply to all company share plans. The company's corporate tax team and the HR and finance teams need to work together on design to ensure effectiveness.

CONCLUSION

The issues discussed above mean cost considerations are a more important part of long-term incentive planning than ever before.

However, this must be weighed against the need to provide an effective incentive for aligning the interests of directors with shareholders and other key stakeholders, and for providing a motivational tool. It will be interesting to see the development of long-term incentive planning in the next year, in light of the new pension tax regime (see part four). Long-term incentive plans could become a more important part of long-term wealth planning.

PART FOUR: PENSIONS

Now is a good time to review directors' pensions. Mark Jackson, partner at actuaries and benefit consultants Lane Clark & Peacock, explains why

EXECUTIVE SUMMARY

- pension benefits remain a key recruitment and retention tool for directors but should be seen in the context of the overall remuneration package

- final salary schemes are increasingly expensive for the employer

- tax changes from April 2006 have profound implications for executive pensions

- remuneration committees need to discuss changes to pensions policy

When key individuals are thinking about moving jobs, maintaining the level of retirement benefits is often a big factor. Directors will want to know that their pension provision is not significantly out of line with market provision. It is important, however, to think of pensions as deferred pay. As such, they form just one element (albeit a major one) of a director's total reward package.

In benchmarking, attention should be paid to each director's total rewards. Where one company offers a less generous pension package, there might be a more significant target bonus to make up for it. This could mean that two companies are, in effect, delivering the same overall value to the executive.

It is advisable for remuneration committees to communicate the value of pension provision regularly. Companies should consider demonstrating the value of the retirement benefits in the context of the overall package.

A TYPICAL PENSION FOR A DIRECTOR

Historically, a typical executive director has earned a final salary pension of one thirtieth of basic salary for each year of service (or two thirds of basic salary after 20 years), payable from a retirement age of 60. The benefit is likely to be largely index linked in payment, and offer a spouse's pension of a half or two-thirds of the director's pension in the event of death.

The final salary pension, however, is proving increasingly expensive to provide. The reasons for this are well-publicised:

- *investment returns are expected to be lower during periods of lower global inflation, producing lower yields on government stocks and higher annuity costs*

- *life expectancy continues to improve, again pushing up the cost of providing pensions*

Many final salary schemes for the wider workforce have closed, and directors have felt this wind of change, particularly when changing employer. There is evidence of a two-tier structure in pension provision for directors. While directors long established in their posts typically enjoy final salary benefits, recently appointed directors are more likely to be offered money purchase benefits, or indeed a salary supplement in lieu of a pension.

The differences between final salary benefits and the alternatives in terms of cost to the employer can be marked. The chart on page 53 shows one of the results of the Lane Clark & Peacock 2004 Survey of Pension Benefits for Executive Directors, which covers companies in the FTSE 100 and FTSE mid 250.

Companies, and directors themselves, need to be fully aware of these potential differences when negotiating a new contract and ensure that the whole remuneration package, including pensions, is hitting the target.

THE NEW TAX REGIME

Currently, there are limits to the pension that can be paid from a tax approved pension scheme. From April 6, 2006, so-called 'A day' when a new tax regime will be introduced, there will be no limit on the amount of pension that a company can provide through its approved pension arrangements.

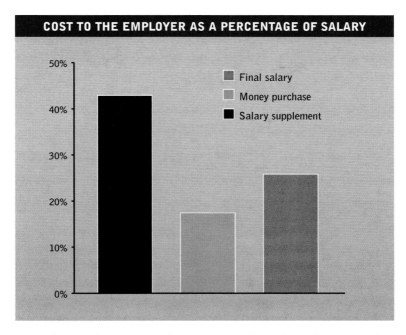

COST TO THE EMPLOYER AS A PERCENTAGE OF SALARY

Legend:
- Final salary
- Money purchase
- Salary supplement

There will, however, be a limit to the value of pension that is provided before an additional tax charge is incurred. Known as the lifetime allowance (LTA), this limit has been set at £1.5m for 2006/07.

There is also an annual limit to the increase in the value of defined benefit rights and contributions under defined contribution arrangements. This limit, £215,000 for 2006/07, will be known as the annual allowance. (It will not apply in the tax year that the benefits are taken in full.) If the annual allowance is exceeded, a tax charge is incurred at the individual's marginal tax rate.

Pensions already earned in excess of the LTA before A day can be protected from the tax charge by registering them. There are two options:

- *enhanced protection – under this, all accrued pension is protected in full and no further tax charge can be incurred. However, no further pension accrual is permitted in the tax approved scheme*

- *primary protection – under this option, each individual is given a personal LTA based on the extent to which their benefits exceed the LTA on A day. Further pension accrual is permitted, but it is likely that tax charges will be incurred*

POLICY VERSUS INDIVIDUAL PROMISES

Since directors have varying levels of pension benefits from current and former pension schemes they will be affected by the new LTA to varying degrees. In addition, those directors for whom enhanced protection is appropriate will need to be compensated for future pension outside of a registered (ie. tax approved) pension scheme.

While applying a common pension policy to all is desirable, in practice it will be difficult to achieve without upsetting some directors. However, some key 'policy' decisions can be taken:

- *should directors be compensated for any additional tax on their pension?*
  Many employers currently reason that the answer should be no: you do not compensate directors for increases to other personal taxes; why make an exception for pensions? Even so, the changes are prompting employers and remuneration committees to review their policy on pensions as the new taxation regime is a radically different framework

- *what level of cash alternative should be offered (if any)?*
  This option is simple and flexible and instantly removes the company's liability. It is tax deductible for the employer but taxable on the employee at receipt. The director is free to decide how it is invested as part of wider retirement planning. Other forms of longer term compensation could be used instead of cash

- *what form of unapproved pension arrangement should be offered (if any)?*
  The taxation of Funded Unapproved Retirement Benefit Schemes (FURBS) is changing and, as a result, FURBS do not look particularly attractive for future contributions

DEFINED BENEFIT V DEFINED CONTRIBUTION

There are two major categories of pension plan: defined benefit (sometimes called final salary schemes) and defined contribution (or money purchase plans)

Defined benefit
A defined benefit plan usually promises to provide a pension calculated as a specified fraction of remuneration in the years close to giving up the directorship (together with death benefits or ill-health retirement benefits). The rate is guaranteed, irrespective of the director's own contributions or, if the scheme is funded, the investment return.

Defined contribution
Under a defined contribution plan, contributions paid in respect of, and by, the director are invested, generally in accordance with principles agreed by the director himself. The director's 'pot' accumulates until retirement (or death), at which point the proceeds are used to buy an annuity (which may include provision for a widow(er)'s pension). The pension amount will depend on both the investment return until the purchase of the annuity and annuity rates at that time. The company provides no guarantee of the amount of pension.

Hybrid schemes
Some 'hybrid' schemes operate as defined benefit or defined contribution schemes, but with an 'underpin'. This means that, if the pension accruing from the defined contribution 'pot' outweighs the guaranteed defined benefit rate, or vice versa, the higher will be paid.

How do you choose?
The individual has greater control over his/her own defined contribution pension accrual. Because of the longer period of compound investment return, the plan could benefit younger members more. For the company, liability is restricted to a fixed percentage of the director's current pensionable remuneration. This often makes the communication of the value of pension in the context of a director's overall package more transparent than under a defined benefit plan.

Under defined benefit plans, the company promises to deliver a benefit based on an unknown future remuneration, with that benefit then guaranteed until the director's death. This promise can lead to unpredictable pension costs, particularly if investment returns are volatile or the individual receives significant pay increases close to retirement. However, most directors attach a high value to the defined benefit promise and it continues to be the chosen method of delivery, especially where this is the norm amongst the company's competitors.

NON-PENSION BENEFITS

In common with most middle and senior managers, executives normally receive a number of benefits provided by the company as part of their remuneration package. These typically divide into two types: health, life and other insurance benefits, and perquisites or fringe benefits such as cars, club memberships and extras provided for both business and personal use

Insurance benefits

The principal insured benefits typically provided to an executive include:

■ Private medical insurance – for the executive, spouse and dependent children.

■ Permanent health insurance – this may be supplementary to ill-health pension arrangements within a defined benefit pension plan. It provides additional cover if the executive is unable to work through ill health up to normal retirement age.

■ Life insurance – this may be supplementary to life cover in a company pension plan and typically includes all salary.

Perquisites

With tax on benefits generally rising, many organisations are reviewing their approach to the more peripheral elements in the benefits package. It is not unusual for companies to offer directors a cash alternative to a benefit, or a flexible benefits programme in which employees can choose the benefits they want within a fixed budgetary amount. The common perquisites provided, or which form part of a benefits 'menu', are:

■ Holidays.

■ A company car – typically, executives may be able to 'trade up' or 'trade down', or take cash.

■ Fuel – many executives with a company car still have all private and business fuel paid for by the company. (This is a highly taxed benefit.)

■ A chauffeur-driven car – this is a far less common benefit and, even in large FTSE 100 companies, may be exclusive to the CEO and chairman. A chauffeured car for business use is a more common large-company benefit.

■ Club membership – these days, this may be a sports gym rather than one of the old-style London clubs.

Additionally, some executives required to work at more than one location may have some housing costs met by the company.

Unfunded Unapproved Retirement Benefit Schemes (UURBS) are a promise to pay an appropriate level of pension directly by the employer at retirement. UURBS are largely unaffected by the new tax regime and so, in theory at least, continue to be a viable option

A director is taxed on UURBS payments at the point payments are received. From the director's point of view, UURBS do have the risk of non payment in the event that the employer defaults (for example due to insolvency or as part of a commercial dispute)

■ *should a notional earnings cap (appropriately indexed) be continued?*
Currently, the maximum level of pensionable earnings is £102,000 for the tax year 2004/05. Under the new tax regime, the earnings cap will be phased out. However, offering the current level of benefits on uncapped earnings will increase costs

COMMUNICATION WITH DIRECTORS

Part of the challenge for remuneration committees in the run up to the introduction of the new tax regime is to communicate any change in pension policy to directors. Each director will be affected by change in their own way. One-to-one sessions with directors are likely to be necessary; this should be borne in mind when planning for change over the period to April 2006.

PART FIVE: THE CONTRACT

Caroline Pugh at law firm Lawrence Graham LLP, looks at the key issues to note when drawing up the executive employment contract

EXECUTIVE SUMMARY

■ the contract must set out the terms of agreement for both executive and company in all possible circumstances – including potential problems

■ tax issues and bonus schemes can cause contractual difficulties

■ employers should avoid including share option promises within employment contracts, as the value of the benefit cannot be guaranteed

■ damages payable for dismissal are now in excess of £50,000

THE TWO IMPERATIVES

From a contractual perspective, there are two imperatives when negotiating the terms of a director's remuneration package.

First, the terms of the agreement must be absolutely clear. A common failing in contracts is that parties elect to postpone difficult decisions in the hope that they will never have to make them. Unfortunately, in the real world, tricky situations demanding difficult decisions often arise. Therefore, when the contract is being negotiated, the parties should, so far as possible, agree what happens under the contract in all circumstances, whether good or bad.

Second, all parties must understand the value of any termination package that the executive may be entitled to – and how that value will be calculated. In the UK, termination packages are directly linked to the length of any notice period that has been agreed and – in circumstances other than summary dismissal on the grounds of gross misconduct – the notice period is the basis for any compensation calculation (see box opposite).

As a rule of thumb, the longer the notice period, the higher the level of damages payable if the executive is asked to leave without working his or her notice.

CHECKLIST FOR AN EXECUTIVE EMPLOYMENT CONTRACT

In any contract for a senior executive there are some core clauses. Particular care should be taken around restrictive covenants and confidentiality provisions as any overly restrictive provisions to protect legitimate business interests may be struck down in their entirety

Every contract should cover the following:

- **Start date** Include statement of continuous period of employment.

- **Termination provisions**
  - Notice period;
  - Compensation payment for immediate termination;
  - Immediate resignation from directorship;
  - Garden leave (if appropriate);
  - Post-termination restrictions (if appropriate);
  - Triggers for summary termination.

- **Job description/duties** The clause should be broad enough to cover the range of duties an executive may be required to perform.

- **Place of work** Include provision for travel in the course of duties (if appropriate)

- **Remuneration package**
  - Statement of fee/salary;
  - Salary review provisions;
  - Pension scheme provisions (including information in relation to contracting out certificate);
  - Bonus and long-term incentive plans;
  - Benefits package including private medical insurance/life assurance/company car, etc.

- **Expenses** Is there a limit on the expenses that the executive can run up without prior authorisation?

- **Holiday entitlement** As a minimum must satisfy the Working Time Regulations

- **Sickness absence** How long will the company pay salary during absences on grounds of illness and how does this interact with any permanent health insurance?

- **Confidentiality provisions** A clause defining the sort of things that are secret in this specific business has a better chance of providing legal protection than a general clause

- **Intellectual property provisions** Does everything belong to the company, or is the executive entitled to benefit personally from some inventions?

For senior executives in public companies, the most common notice period is 12 months; any shorter and it may be difficult to recruit or retain staff; any longer and there will be challenging conversations with investors.

It is becoming increasingly common for contracts to have shorter notice periods of, say, six months, which are activated if the director chooses to resign. This obviously reduces the potential damages payable if the company decides not to require the director to work the full period.

COMMON PROBLEMS

bonus schemes

Bonus schemes broadly fall into two categories: those that provide guaranteed and measurable benefits on the satisfaction of specific targets; those that give the remuneration committee broad discretion. In the past, many companies assumed they could exercise this discretion how they liked, but it's now clear that the courts require them to act in a reasonable way. This point comes up most often on termination, where a company may be required to make a payment in respect of an allegedly discretionary bonus, with the remuneration committee obliged to exercise its discretion in the way it would have done had the executive remained employed.

taxation

One law that is sometimes overlooked in contracts is section 311 of the Companies Act. This makes it unlawful for a company to agree to pay a director a net salary. This provision is designed to prevent a company effectively agreeing to absorb a director's personal tax liability by guaranteeing to pay whatever amount provides an income of £x.

long-term incentives

Long-term incentives can cause problems where the value of the benefit provided is less than expected. As a matter of good practice, employers should seek to keep long-term incentive promises out of employment contracts. Entitlements arising from long-term incentives should be treated in accordance with the rules of the incentives scheme, rather than under a parallel employment right that may have been inadvertently created in an employment contract.

poor performance

The fact that the payment of damages is based upon the notice period means that executives who are dismissed for poor performance can still receive substantial pay offs.

Remuneration committees of public companies must consider the best way of minimising any compensation payment to an executive in these circumstances. As well as the traditional argument that payment should be reduced to reflect likely mitigation, it may also be possible to vary notice periods according to the reason for a director's dismissal. For example, a contract may provide that the notice period in circumstances of redundancy is 12 months, but that if the reason for the dismissal is that the company has under-performed (by reference to clear criteria agreed at the outset), it may be shortened to three. This is not yet common practice among public companies but may find favour with the increasing number of remuneration committees that are eager to minimise the size of payments to executives who have added little or no value to the business.

summary dismissal

Poor performance is almost never a ground for summary dismissal without payment of compensation. The only exception would be where the actions of the director were effectively negligent, or where the contract sets out very clear and specific performance criteria that have not been met. However, even if a contract entitles summary dismissal on the grounds of specific poor performance, it is likely that any termination would be deemed an 'unfair dismissal' unless the executive had been warned that his performance might result in sacking and was given a reasonable chance to improve.

Chapter 5

Reporting

PART ONE: COMPLIANCE

Jarrod Simpson, company secretarial partner at Ernst & Young, lists the main disclosure rules for directors' pay

EXECUTIVE SUMMARY

- the rulebook is long and, in parts, complicated; expert professional advice might be needed

- companies need to comply with statutory rules and any further provisions under the Stock Exchange Listing rules and the Combined Code

- the remuneration report must include for each director not only a retrospective account of pay but also a statement of the company's future intentions

Quoted companies must comply with reporting requirements for directors' remuneration; non-compliance can result in fines.

The requirements fall into three categories:

- *statutory (those required by the Companies Acts)*

- *regulatory (those required under the Listing Rules of the UK Listing Authority)*

- *best practice (as set out by the Combined Code on Corporate Governance, which is appended to the Listing Rules).*

There is some overlap between the categories and some duplication of provisions. This chapter outlines the main requirements.

STATUTORY RULES

As previous chapters have said, the statutory rules were amended in 2002 by the Directors' Remuneration Report Regulations. The rules apply to companies quoted on the Official List (with the exception of AIM stocks), an official list of a European Economic Area state and the NYSE and Nasdaq.

They stipulate that a directors' remuneration report, approved by the board and signed on its behalf, must be circulated in the same way as the annual report and accounts and laid before a general meeting. At the meeting, shareholders must be given the right to a separate advisory vote on the remuneration report.

The remuneration report must include the names of each director who was or had been a member of the remuneration committee and specific information on and about the use of any remuneration consultants. It must also include:

- *a forward-looking policy statement on the remuneration of directors, giving, for each director:*

i. *a summary of any performance conditions relating to any entitlement to share options under a long-term incentive scheme;*

ii. *an explanation of why those conditions were selected;*

iii. *a summary of the methods to be used in determining whether those conditions are met;*

iv. *information about any external factors used to compare performance, and, where those factors relate to other companies or an index, the identity of the other companies or index;*

v. *a description and explanation of any proposed significant amendment relating to the entitlement of any director to share options under a long-term incentive scheme;*

vi. *an explanation of why entitlements to share options under a long-term incentive scheme are not subject to performance conditions, if that is the case;*

vii. *an explanation of the relative importance of each element in the remuneration package that is performance-linked;*

viii. *an explanation of the company's policy on specific aspects of service contracts.*

- *a line graph comparing the company's share price performance (by reference to total shareholder return, fairly calculated according to specified criteria) with that of other shares on a named equity market index, over a five-year period. (The company must explain why the particular comparator index has been chosen)*

■ *facts about the service contracts of each director, including: the date of the contract; the unexpired term; notice periods; provision for compensation on early termination, together with information necessary to estimate liability in the event of early termination*

■ *a breakdown of the remuneration packages for each named director into: basic salary and fees (including 'golden hellos'); bonuses; expenses allowances and benefits in kind (those chargeable to UK income tax); compensation for loss of office and/or other payments connected with early termination or breach of contract; other non-cash benefits not falling under one of the prescribed heads. The amounts must be totalled and appear in tabular form, together with comparisons on the previous year. The nature and the estimated value of 'other non-cash benefits' must also be stated*

■ *a policy statement on the granting of executive options or awards under any SAYE or other long-term incentive scheme. (Any departure from or change to the previous year's policy must be explained and justified)*

■ *disclosure of share options and SAYE options for each director, as at the end of the financial year and until a date not more than one month before the circulation of the annual report and accounts.*
Total interests must be shown and a distinction should be made between those that are beneficial and those that are non-beneficial. (Beneficial shares are those held either in the director's name or the name of a person or persons 'connected' to him – eg. spouse, child – or held by a company controlled by him or a 'connected person').

The following must be disclosed:

i *share options that were awarded or exercised in the year;*

ii   share options that expired unexercised in the year;

iii   any variation to the terms and conditions relating to the award or exercise of share options.

For all unexpired share options disclosure is required of:

i   the price paid for the award, the exercise price (if applicable);

ii   the date from which the options may be exercised and the date on which they expire;

iii   the market price at the end of the year and the highest and lowest prices during that year. (Certain aggregation is permitted to avoid excessive length, but this is a complicated area of disclosure, requiring professional help.)

■   details of each director's interests in any long-term incentive schemes (other than share options) at both the start and the end of the year under review. Entitlements and awards granted during the year must also be made public, and the year in which they can be taken up, together with any variations made to any scheme terms

■   details of contributions to and entitlements in any defined benefit pension scheme for each director, along with the amount of retirement benefits accruing in the year, the accumulated accrued benefits (pension and lump sum) as at the end of the year under review, information on or necessary to determine transfer values, early retirement rights and any discretionary benefits

■   for money purchase pension schemes, details of contributions made or payable during the year under review

■   disclosure of the aggregate of excess retirement benefits receivable by directors, past directors or their nominees or dependents

■   disclosure of significant payments made to former directors during the year

■   disclosure of the aggregate of consideration payable to third *parties for the services of any director. (Details of the esti-mated money value and the nature of any non-cash benefits must be given.)*

- *an explanation of and justification for any element of remu-neration that is pensionable other than basic salary*

- *a distinction between those amounts paid for services as a director of a company or its subsidiaries, and those paid under a contract of employment, either with the company or its subsidiaries. A director of a parent company must also disclose in the parent company's accounts amounts of emoluments paid to him/her by subsidiaries*

- *disclosure of the 'aggregate amount of directors' emoluments etc', as required under para 1, schedule 6 of the Companies Act 1985*

REGULATORY RULES (LISTING RULES)

In broad terms, Rule 12.43A(c) of the UK Listing Rules mirrors in many areas the provisions of the Directors' Remuneration Report Regulations, detailed above.

In one or two areas, the Listing Rules impose obligations on listed companies that go beyond those set out by the statutory rules. These are paragraphs 12.43A(c)(v) and 12.43A(c)(ix)(b) on directors' pensions. Listed companies will need to comply with both the provisions set out in the statutory rules and any additional requirements laid down by the Listing Rules.

BEST PRACTICE

The new Combined Code on Corporate Governance, published by the Financial Reporting Council, excludes material in the previous Code on the disclosure of directors' remuneration. This is because by the time it was published in July 2003, the new Directors' Remuneration Report Regulations 2002 were already in force.

The new Code does, however, make the following additional requirements, compliance with which must be indicated in the reports and accounts:

- *where a company releases an executive director to serve as a non-executive director elsewhere, the remuneration report should include a statement as to whether or not the director will retain his remuneration from this external appointment and, if so, what that remuneration is*

- *the remuneration committee should make available its terms of reference, explaining its role and the authority delegated to it by the board. (As chapter 2 made clear, this requirement is met either by making the information available on request or by including it on the company's website)*

- *shareholders should be asked to approve all new long-term incentive schemes (as defined in the Listing Rules), and significant changes to existing schemes, save in the circumstances permitted by the Listings Rules*

PART TWO: INVESTOR AND MEDIA RELATIONS

Careful management can avert clashes with shareholders and help avoid bad publicity

EXECUTIVE SUMMARY

- the new disclosure rules mean that information about remuneration can no longer be buried; the 'bad' board will be exposed

- companies must understand and respect the concerns of shareholders

- effective and timely consultation with investors will minimise the risk of adverse votes

- the sensible company will anticipate remuneration-related questions at the AGM and have answers prepared

Earlier chapters of this guide have referred to tougher disclosure rules and to closer scrutiny – by both investors and journalists – of decisions relating to executive remuneration. It is essential that remuneration committees consider the impact on investor relations of their policies and remember the media appetite for 'fat cat' exposés.

The amount of information that must, by law, be set out in the directors' report on remuneration has significantly increased. Before the introduction of the new reporting regulations, some details could be fudged: now there is a set of prescribed rules for what must be included in the remuneration report. Over the last two reporting seasons, most companies appear to have accepted the new regime.

Ernst & Young research into voting recommendations by ABI's Institutional Voting Information Service (IVIS) and NAPF's Research Recommendations Electronic Voting (RREV) has shown that only five per cent of published remuneration reports for years ending on or after September 30, 2004 were regarded by shareholders as non-compliant.

RESPECTING SHAREHOLDERS

Management of executive remuneration is not just about legal compliance, but also about understanding and respecting the views of investors. Shareholder representative organisations (such as ABI, NAPF and PIRC) publish guidelines on executive remuneration. And individual shareholders are making their views clearer.

Remuneration committees should bear the guidelines of institutional investors in mind when drawing up policies. It might be that a proposed remuneration policy is in line with the guidelines of one or two institutions, but not the third: the sensible committee will prepare sound arguments for non-compliance; it will build a robust, respectful case for its defence.

SHAREHOLDER CONCERNS

Awareness of the concerns of shareholders will help companies spot any potential problems with remuneration policies and practices. The key issues highlighted by the two voter advisory organisations referred to above are (in order of frequency):

- *independence of non-executive directors*
- *performance conditions for long-term incentive plans*
- *aspects of the design or operation of long-term incentives*
- *contractual terms – principally contract duration and change of control provisions*

independence of non-executive directors

The independence of non-executive directors was a concern before the publication of the revised Combined Code, but the new Code has added weight to the case made by institutional investors. The key tests of independence are whether non-executives:

- *have served on the board for longer than nine years*
- *have previously been executive directors of the company or have had another close relationship with it*

In some companies, non-executive directors who were not independent had lower votes in favour of their re-election in 2004.

69

performance conditions

Shareholders continue to express concern regarding the stretch (or lack of it) required for the vesting of long-term incentives. In 2004, shareholders particularly opposed re-testing, which effectively gives executives another bite at the share plan cherry if performance targets are not met. Shareholder attitudes are hardening. The common requirements of shareholders are that:

■ *plans do not have re-testing opportunities*

■ *awards should not vest for below 'median', or satisfactory performance*

■ *performance comparator groups are appropriately structured*

A 'zero-tolerance' approach to re-testing is expected in 2005.

other long-term incentive issues

Quantum and design concerns continue. Disapproval is at its highest where performance conditions are perceived to be unchallenging or in those (now rare) cases where there are no performance conditions at all. Other general concerns include:

■ *uncapped share awards*

■ *inadequate disclosure*

■ *awards of shares at levels above normal market practice*

contracts and severance payments

Companies' policies have changed following sustained shareholder pressure to limit executive contracts to one year and to reduce payments made on severance following a change of control. The vast majority of companies complied with institutional shareholder guidelines on these matters in 2004; those that did not were generally censured.

MAINTAINING GOOD RELATIONS

As well as observing institutional guidelines, companies can take a number of practical steps to reduce the likelihood of adverse comments, or votes against remuneration reports.

consultation

When planning a new remuneration policy – particularly if it involves potentially controversial practices – it pays to hold informal talks with individual institutions and the representative organisations. The chairman of the remuneration committee should lead the meeting from the company's perspective with support from the human resources director, company secretary, or external remuneration advisers. This gives the remuneration committee the chance to understand possible objections, and how to deal with them. By creating a forum of mutual respect and understanding, it improves the chances of support. It does not mean backing down on decisions; it means helping shareholders to understand them.

careful preparation of the report

Before the AGM, remuneration policy and details will be published in the directors' report on remuneration. The new regulations direct that the report should be more than a retrospective of remuneration details: the future intention of the company should be described in a remuneration policy statement. It is essential that sufficient time is spent on preparing the report. Reporting is not merely a compliance exercise: it should be seen as a PR opportunity to present accurately future remuneration arrangements. Shareholders will vote on the report at the AGM; a vote against the company will form the basis of media commentary.

anticipation of questions

Consultation before the AGM should give the company an idea of what to expect at the meeting. However, there might be a number of issues that give rise to media interest, and the emotive subject of remuneration can easily be "tagged on". Thorough preparation for likely questions on remuneration can reinforce the fact that the committee has conscientiously debated the issues and constructed a robust remuneration policy.

CONCLUSION

The presentation of the remuneration policy is a critical challenge for companies. If it is done well, very little attention should be drawn to it. Companies should be prepared for a disproportionate level of interest if the communication of remuneration practice and policy is mishandled. Remuneration has become a PR minefield for companies, with no shortage of commentators jumping on the bandwagon. Compliance with guidelines alone is no longer sufficient to avoid adverse publicity; careful handling of remuneration issues is becoming increasingly important.

Chapter 6

The future

Rises in executive pay continue to hit the headlines. But, says business author and journalist Carol Kennedy, the days of boardroom indulgence could be numbered

EXECUTIVE SUMMARY

- regulatory changes mean remcos are under new pressure to justify their decisions
- international accounting standards are helping to force changes in the make-up of executive pay packages
- institutional shareholders are proving effective 'pay police' and are asking for further reform
- differences in pay rises for executives and employees are increasingly being called into question

There are still, inescapably, two nations in the business world. The earnings gap between directors and employees is widening, and where pensions are concerned, chief executives live on another planet from the many who now face a lean retirement. But some of the extra cream that has been heaped on the senior executive cake in recent years, notably in share options and severance deals, is already being scooped off by new accounting rules and shorter service contracts.

Accelerating this trend is a much more sceptical shareholder attitude to any assumption that an expensive CEO deserves their wealth, in the words of that L'Oreal slogan, "because I'm worth it".

Added to which, there is new pressure to ensure the integrity and objectivity of the remuneration committee. The new Combined Code incorporating Sir Derek Higgs's recommendations on non-executive responsibilities requires companies to exclude chairmen (no longer regarded as independent) from audit or remuneration committees. Currently, one in four chairmen in the FTSE

100 sit on such committees, and time is running out for their replacement by independents.

THE UPWARD SPIRAL

The intensified scrutiny on how executive pay is decided is likely to focus on more than a few headline cases of lavishly rewarded CEOs. A recent survey of the leading 350 listed companies by Income Data Services (IDS) found that directors' pay as a whole rose by 16 per cent in 2003, while a similar study by the *Guardian* put the figure at 13 per cent. Other research groups such as the Pensions and Investment Research Consultants (PIRC), looking at executive teams as a whole, suggest a more modest increase of between five and ten per cent, although that could rise to 20 per cent depending on what bonuses and other perks are included.

The big leap in 2003, according to IDS, came in annual cash bonuses, totalling 76 per cent of FTSE 350 salaries, up from 64 per cent the previous year. The National Association of Pension Funds (NAPF), which is said to control about a fifth of the UK stockmarket, finds that maximum annual bonus levels have soared from 60 per cent of salary to 100 per cent.

NAPF, which recently set up a service to advise members on voting at AGMs, fully backs the principle of rewards for performance, but its research specialist Chris Niland says most companies are cagey about disclosing how the targets are met, claiming the information is "price-sensitive".

FORCES FOR CHANGE

Yet remuneration committees are certainly being forced into rethinking the wider ramifications of their decisions. A number of new factors are behind this, led by a spate of governance guidelines from the International Corporate Governance Network (ICGN), the Higgs review, NAPF and the Association of British Insurers (ABI), the other major UK body representing institutional investors.

In addition, new legislation in 2002 gave shareholders the right to vote on the remuneration report. Although the vote is only advisory, it quickly had an impact on board decisions, notably when GlaxoSmithKline (GSK) was forced to tear up the two-year service contract of its chief executive. A proposed £22m "golden goodbye" for CEO Jean-Pierre Garnier in the event of his leaving the company early was the trigger for a shareholder revolt in May 2003. Garnier's contract is now 12 months.

GSK chairman Sir Christopher Hogg, who had already gone through the fire over remuneration terms for Reuters' new US-recruited chief executive, was obliged to devote two days a week for the best part of a year to hammering out a policy that would satisfy British shareholders as well as meet the pharmaceutical giant's need to compete for international talent.

INTERNATIONAL ACCOUNTING STANDARDS

The third major trigger for change has been international account-ing standards (IAS). Share options granted after November 2002 must now be shown as an expense in the profit and loss account. Although IAS or International Financial Reporting Standards (IFRS) only became 'official' on January 1, 2005, their impact has already been felt.

LENGTH OF CONTRACTS

The most visible sign of the new shareholder activism has been the shortening of service contracts. James Clarke of PIRC says the trend towards shorter contract periods is "the direct result of investor pressure. At one time, three or even five-year periods were normal".

Sir Nigel Mobbs, chairman of Slough Estates, agrees that "we are all on a level playing field now as far as contracts are con-cerned. Everyone is striving to bring them down to 12 months". But he has always been sceptical about shareholder voting on remuneration. "I don't think that shareholders always really under-stand the dynamics of remuneration or the circumstances behind them, including those behind longer contracts."

'LEGACY' AWARDS

Meanwhile, chickens are still coming home to roost in 'legacy' cases where contracts were drawn up in a more indulgent environment, notably the beleaguered Sainsbury group, which came under heavy fire in 2004 for allowing a £3m payoff to its ousted CEO, Sir Peter Davis, after the worst losses in the company's 135-year history.

Some of the controversial bonus awards of 2004 may also be classified as legacies, such as the millions granted to the directors of the 'new' Marconi for bringing the company back from the dead – critics would say that was what they were hired to do – and £800,000 paid to six executives at Jarvis, the rail and infrastructure services company, for the year of the Potters Bar rail crash.

SHAREHOLDER INFORMATION, SHAREHOLDER POWER

Enforced transparency is a first step to minimising opportunities for greed.

There is a desire among institutional investors to see change being pushed faster by more activism. "So far, there has been little change in terms of pay packages apart from contracts," observes PIRC's Clarke. "PIRC has called on the government to legislate to allow shareholders the right to approve any payments in excess of six months' salary prior to them being made. Given the occurrence of large payoffs even where contracts are for one year, we think problems in this area will continue.

"I suspect there will be an eventual slowing down in pay rises, as investor attention continues to grow," says Clarke. "Whether the upward spiral will actually stop is harder to predict."

CALL FOR MORE REFORM

Both PIRC and NAPF question whether companies are aware enough of the effects huge pay differentials have on employees' morale. NAPF wants remuneration reports to explain why salary inflation is running at a higher level in the boardroom than elsewhere in the company. NAPF's Chris Niland says: "There needs to be justification for a director that is performing averagely or poorly getting an extra 15 per cent year on year, as opposed to three per cent in line with retail price inflation for the average employee."

For further information contact:

Ernst & Young LLP
Tim Rolfe: 020 7951 6468
Executive compensation team: 020 7951 2000
www.ey.com/uk

Lawrence Graham LLP
Caroline Pugh: 020 7759 6433
www.lawgram.com

Lane Clark & Peacock LLP
Mark Jackson: 020 7439 2266
www.lcp.uk.com

Institute of Directors
020 7839 1233
www.iod.com